Quitting Cold

Quitting Cold

A Guide to Quit Smoking

By Carling Kalicak

iUniverse, Inc.
Bloomington

Quitting Cold
A Guide to Quit Smoking

iUniverse books may be ordered through booksellers or by contacting:

iUniverse
1663 Liberty Drive
Bloomington, IN 47403
www.iuniverse.com
1-800-Authors (1-800-288-4677)

Because of the dynamic nature of the Internet, any Web addresses or links contained in this book may have changed since publication and may no longer be valid. The views expressed in this work are solely those of the author and do not necessarily reflect the views of the publisher, and the publisher hereby disclaims any responsibility for them.

Any people depicted in stock imagery provided by Thinkstock are models, and such images are being used for illustrative purposes only.

Certain stock imagery © Thinkstock.

ISBN: 978-1-4502-8545-2 (sc)
ISBN: 978-1-4502-8546-9 (ebook)
ISBN: 978-1-4502-8547-6 (dj)

Printed in the United States of America

iUniverse rev. date: 2/22/2011

For Chip –
My comrade, thank you for opening my eyes in 2008.

For Shane –
My ally and confidant. You are the reason this book even exists, I couldn't have done it without you.

For mom, dad and my brother you allowed me to be a free spirit and explore life without borders.

In loving memory of my uncle Randy who passed away due to complications with throat cancer.

If one's sword is broken, he will strike with his hands. If his hands are cut off, he will press the enemy down with his shoulders. If his shoulders are cut away he will bite through ten or fifteen enemy necks with his teeth. Courage is such a thing.

— Yamamoto Tsunemoto

Contents

Introduction

WE'VE ALL HEARD THOSE REMARKABLE "I quit cold turkey" stories from our friends, and although we find it incredibly hard to believe, it isn't a myth at all. It's true! Quitting smoking can be accomplished by using willpower. All you need is the proper education and techniques on how to prepare your mind and body for the smoke-free you. Like most smokers, I'm sure the moment you pick up a cigarette, you make a decision to say to yourself "One day I will quit," this initiates a desire to conquer.

Surprisingly, even if you've said it a hundred thousand times already, you are still applying the first step in change: desire.

Today is the eighth official day that I quit smoking and even at eight days I can brag about it. I used to smoke up to sixty cigarettes a day, but conditioned myself to cut it down to zero. This is the first time in my 12 years of smoking that I have been able to quit without the use of nicotine suppressants or over-whelming cravings. Finally, I've conquered this deadly addiction.

After trying over and over again what always seemed to be the hardest was actually the easiest. Wouldn't it be great if you could just wake up one day, quit, and never look back? To be able to say with confidence the first day someone offers you a cigarette, "No thank you. I don't smoke." Well, for you I have outlined the set-backs and strategies that I used to cope and quit.

After having influenced friends, family and strangers with my methods, I am certain that you are no exception and can quit smoking comfortably and naturally.

If you give the techniques laid out in this book an honest attempt, I know it will help you. I've been there, I've tried a thousand times over to quit so I know it's hard but I also know it is 100% possible.

In the end, there are some things we can overcome with the help of others and then there are just some things we each need to solve on our own. In my opinion, quitting tobacco is one of those things. You need to overcome this by yourself. I say this so that someone else's failure doesn't encourage your own. When people quit together most of the time they share the same desire to quit but are at different places in the mind.

If your quitting partner doesn't have the strength to follow through with it they may give up and when they do you will likely give up too. A team effort to quit smoking because you don't feel strong enough to do it alone, is probably one of the biggest reasons why most people never succeed at quitting. You can't base your success off of someone else's.

Here's another bit of food for thought. The only way you'll ever be able to quit nicotine is by not having nicotine of any kind wilfully enter your system e.g. second-hand smoke. When you are ready, if you can avoid nicotine for three weeks, it will be completely out of your system. Once it is out of your system, the rest of the work is building the right frame of mind.

Lastly, no matter how crude this book may get, embarrassment for your actions is a great way to open your mind to change.

CHAPTER ONE

Step One:
Preparing for the
Future

BEFORE WE GET STARTED LET'S discuss how to use this book effectively. First, read the book entirely to grasp the concept. Once you have done that, read through each step again and go at your own pace. Be sure not to move onto the next step in the book, until you are completely comfortable with the step you are currently on. Also note that some of the steps may not apply to your situation therefore move forward to any steps that do. Now, let's get started!

If you're like me then you are tired of hearing people bash smokers and bug you all the time about "When are you going to quit?" Well, you can tell them, that quitting an addiction doesn't happen just like that. It can take months, even years to prepare yourself for it. It has to be done for you by you without any other reason. What should you do if a person counters your logic? You could politely explain to them that, instead of sitting here lying about the fact that you are quitting while you continue to smoke for the next year or two. You are taking the next year or two to enjoy yourself as a smoker and prepare yourself for a smoke-free future. Yes, you heard correctly. You can use this book to quit sooner but if time permits, I want you to smoke for as long as you like (you'll come to understand why). However, if you don't already, every time you light up, the first key to success will be to tell your cigarette, "One of these days I will quit." I know it doesn't make much sense right now but cold turkey is all about psychology.

Now, one of the main concerns smokers have about quitting is the future. They often meet people who say "I quit for 14 years" but now they are a full-time smoker again. This can be very discouraging but what I always say to that is they probably quit for all the wrong reasons. Most will cover it up with an excuse like "I am going through a divorce" or "Somebody close to me just passed away", "I just got a clean bill of health" and the most popular "We are all going to die someday". The way I interpret those is "I quit for my significant other", "Now people won't bother me about my smoking because I am grieving", "I quit because my doctor told me to at the time" and "I relapsed. So, instead of trying to quit again, I'll just hide my guilt behind the inevitable". All these reasons have one thing in common; that the individual wasn't entirely ready to quit in the first place.

The most important key point that I can share, is this one important lesson: you need to substitute your smoking habit with something you enjoy equally as much. As an example, I assumed skipping rope would be my niche. When I was a child it was all I wanted to do. It's also great for ex-smokers as instead of smoking every hour for ten minutes, you can find a private place to skip rope indoors or out. Not only does it take your mind off of smoking, it clears your lungs out and gets you into shape, giving physical results of the new non-smoking you. Might I add that physical results are a great way to keep you motivated and determined to quit? Another great thing about skipping is after. You don't even want a cigarette!

Quitting an addiction doesn't happen overnight. It's just like weight loss. It took years to put on weight, and it could take years to patiently remove the weight. I have found that discovering the right motivation to quit smoking is one of the first important steps to success in building will power.

Let's face it, no one is born with will power; you have to earn it by taking things one day at a time. The road to recovery is best travelled slowly.

Developing enough strength to wilfully end a bad habit can take months, even years to accomplish. Forget planning ahead and picking a quit date. Remember what I said about psychology? Start by telling yourself that tomorrow you are going to quit!

Keys to Success

Lesson one: You must want to quit, discover the motivating factor and substitute it with something you enjoy equally as much.

Keys to Success

Lesson two: You have to earn willpower by taking things one day at a time. Start by telling every cigarette, one day you will quit.

CHAPTER TWO

Step Two:
What Does Your
Cigarette Symbolize

WHAT ROLE DOES YOUR CIGARETTE fill? Is it a friend? Maybe it's an enemy? Then again, it could be your lover or your master. Either way, your cigarette is a manipulative item that has been ripping you off since the day you met.

The third key is recognizing that your cigarette does not own you; you own it! You paid nearly one hour's worth of work for a pack of those ammonia-filled, lung-cringing, urine-tasting sticks that love to suck the life out of you and your skin. Think of it this way, for every pack that stole an hour of your daily wages, took more than just money. It took four hours off your life! That's approximately 1,460 hours, gone per year.

Take a look around you; people can instantly tell who is a smoker and who isn't. What's worse is that every time you spark one up, you look ridiculous with your fingers locked around your life partner, commencing suicide with your lips.

Just like Romeo and Juliet, you and your cigarette share a tragic love with one another. Oh, what a faithful friend; a friend who never lets you down. The one who supports you when you're having emotional bouts of any kind—except when those emotional bouts are in regards to not being able to smoke when you want to; then things tend to get ugly.

Will that same friend come to comfort you when you are hacking up a lung, unable to breathe, and choking on your own mucus? How about your beauty? Will it allow you to shine and be natural at twenty and older, or will you cover up with pounds of makeup, Botox injections and cosmetic surgery? Does that same friend make you smell more attractive for a date or frighten them away? What I am trying to say is that not only do you let your cigarette own you, but you wear its effects clearly even when you try to hide it.

Keys to Success
    Lesson three: Your cigarette does not own you; you own it.

Keys to Success

Lesson four: You wear its effects clearly even when you try to hide it.

CHAPTER THREE

Step Three:
Saying No

IT IS NOW TIME THAT you learned to tell your brain you are boss and one of these days when it's least expecting it, you are going to nip this habit in the bud.

Start your days off by not reaching for your morning cigarette; wake up, go use the john, do your hair and your makeup, bathe, shave, and so on. Just do something, anything, for at least one hour before you spark up your morning breath of fresh air. Once you're comfortable with that for at least one or two weeks, try bumping it up to two hours and so on and so forth. After you have mastered the morning smoke, try doing the same with your before bed smoke.

Here is something else to consider: I don't care how cold it is outside in the winter or how suffocating and hot it can be in the summer. Don't smoke in the house or your vehicle! If you smoke inside an enclosed area, you have to break this habit. You are much too comfortable with your habit and need to start divorcing tobacco from your personal and professional life, for example while driving, reading, watching tv, drinking coffee or alcohol, when you first wake up, or immediately before bed. Also try to make subtle changes at work such as limiting how many cigarettes you smoke per break and eventually skipping a smoke-break all together. Learn to adapt (one step at a time) to your current lifestyle without always having a cigarette as a form of reward, stress reliever or for the sake of something to do.

If you have kids and smoke around them, then this is a great place to start. Vow to never smoke when the kids are around. Also don't smoke while standing in front of public entranceways or other places where people may find walking through your cloud of toxin to be repulsive.

Do yourself a favour and start to feel embarrassed and ashamed about smoking, acknowledge that it truthfully is a disgusting habit. I used to be so arrogant that I believed the ban on smoking in public places was taking freedom away from others. Now, I realize that non-smokers shouldn't have to accept smokers; smokers should have to accept the fact that more and more people want to live a long, healthy life. You were the one who made the choice to do something that is un-healthy and un-natural so respect the general public around you. We all know we're going to die one day, but try to appreciate the decision non-smokers make. Understand that more and more people are making healthier choices every day. Inhaling your wafting cloud of smoke is not on their agenda.

Keys to Success

Lesson five: Start your day off without lighting up for one hour. Reduce how many cigarettes you smoke on break and or skip a smoke-break all together.

Keys to Success

Lesson six: Don't smoke in the house or car.

Keys to Success

Lesson seven: Feel embarrassed and ashamed about smoking.

CHAPTER FOUR

Step Four:

Gaining Your Privacy Back

Now that you have gained control by cutting back on critical habit points, it is time to start becoming a non-smoker.

Get cleaning! After you stop smoking in the car or house, I want you to wash all the nicotine off the walls of either your car or home. Do you notice something different? After some time has passed whenever you now enter your car or home after having a cigarette, the smell of you is going to hit like a bag of bricks. Not to mention the discovery of unpleasant odours coming from the clean clothes in your closet; fibres reeking from chemical stains just like the ones that have developed inside of your organs. In fact, you will notice that anytime you enter a structure, whether it is a place of work, a movie theatre, a restaurant, or a mall after having a smoke, the understanding of why non-smokers dislike this habit so much will become shockingly clear. You stink!

Your nose will improve so much just from eliminating enclosed smoking that when fellow smoking colleagues come to join you for a meeting, their stench will be so over whelming that you will actually feel bad for them. Gum, perfume, mouthwash, coffee, and toothpaste don't really help. They just mix with the tobacco smell and make the odour worse!

Once you experience something similar it will begin to trigger true feelings of guilt. At one point you only said you felt ashamed to be a smoker, but now you actually feel it. Soon you'll be questioning when and where you will be able to smoke and how long you need to air off to reduce embarrassment. This is highly important. Use it to your advantage, and allow the guilt in to help motivate your spirit and strengthen your will power!

Keys to Success

Lesson eight: Wash the nicotine from your life.

Keys to Success

Lesson nine: Allow the guilt in and use it to build will power.

CHAPTER FIVE

Step Five:

Now is the Time
to Quit

YOU GET IT; YOU'RE AFRAID, you are constantly worried, and you are becoming paranoid. Now that you can see through the eyes of a non-smoker just how terrible smoking looks on the outside, I'm sure you are probably asking "What's on the inside?" It is time for you to calm down. You are going to quit, remember? It doesn't matter how long it has taken you to reach this step in the book; the point is you are finally here and now you want out.

From today until the day you quit, every Monday that comes your way is your new quit day. To set your expectations for every single Monday without skipping a beat, you are going to tell yourself the day before "Today is Sunday and tomorrow I am going to give it a fair and honest try." I must let you in on a secret though: you're still not ready to quit just yet.

This next step requires you to go on out to your pharmacy and pick yourself up some nicotine gum. No, you may not get the patch. For this step you may only use the gum or lozenges. I will explain why. With nicotine patches you are constantly pumping nicotine into your system. When you get a craving, what will you do with it? Bite your tongue? Chew some gum? Rip the patch off and have a smoke? Needless to say the patch overlooks the oral satisfaction of smoking. Now, let's talk about nicotine suppressant inhalers; can you say encouraging the habit? Inhalers can be used with the gum if you just need that finger fix, but I only suggest you use it at maximum twice per day. Remember the goal is to break the habits associated with smoking.

I recommend using the gum because it allows your body to be in a natural state for long periods of time in between cravings and comes in many flavours (my personal favourite was citrus). However, the gum will only work when it is used as directed. If used as directed (bite-bite park) within twenty minutes you will find that you no longer crave a cigarette.

After you have substituted Monday's for Gumdays and some time has passed you will notice one thing. The gum more than likely will begin to hurt your mouth and tongue, which leads you to start fearing the gum. This is a masterpiece in itself. Once you fear the gum, you automatically cringe at the thought of having it; this encourages you to wait until you absolutely, positively, must have nicotine. The feeling of dislike is groundbreaking because this is where you are truly going to learn how to cope with cravings. If you like, at the end of each Gum-day reward yourself with one cigarette and make sure it is at night, never in the morning. Smoking in the morning will make you want to smoke throughout the day, if you do this you are setting yourself up for an automatic fail. This technique is what you will resort to every Monday that you quit.

Keys to Success

Lesson ten: Substitute Monday for Gum-day's.

Keys to Success

Lesson eleven: Reward yourself with one smoke at the end of your Gum-day but only in the evening.

CHAPTER SIX

Step Six:

Antsy with the Gum

FORTUNATELY YOU WON'T BE COMPLETELY antsy. That's the beauty with gum. Not only are you learning how to survive without hand to mouth motions, but you are curbing your cravings while developing more energy from not actually smoking. What does that mean? Have fun with it! Start to look at your cravings as a high. The truth is that more oxygen is in fact reaching your brain, so while you're thinking that the temporary lightness of the world is a craving coming on, it is actually your brain adjusting to the new blasts of oxygen it never had before. That'd make anybody's head spin for sure!

It is natural when you have smoked for so long and have quit (even for a day) to perceive things as being fuzzy and to feel light-headed. Don't be scared though. Enjoy it; your body is not used to this kind of enjoyment; I promise this is one high that won't cost you anything especially not money, a prison sentence, or further risk of physical harm.

Just as a reminder, take this information in and apply it even if all you're able to do is quit one Monday a week and by Tuesday you're smoking again. Give yourself a pat on the back. The real trick is making honest attempts to stay committed to the game of learning how to cope with stressful situations and nicotine withdrawals. Not to mention your success in everything accomplished up to this point.

Once you are comfortable with one Gum-day, try substituting two, and eventually three days out of the week. Before you know it those two to three days will become two to three weeks. Often people state that the first three days of quitting are the worst to get through but I say the first day is.

For this reason, I'd rather see you go an entire day without having a smoke because it exposes and familiarizes you with the reality of quitting. However, like I said, if the cravings are really bothering you during those trial periods, allow yourself to have one smoke a day.

Just, in case you are wondering if these methods are safe. It has been reported by the makers of quit aids that nicotine gum can be used to cut back (meaning you can still smoke, just not at the same time or directly after). The patch can still have adverse effects. Always remember you are trying to quit. Don't take advantage of the situation; try and give yourself a fair and honest chance each and every time you use the gum.

Besides, what other guide to quitting smoking would tell you to smoke as part of the program?

Keys to Success

Lesson twelve: Replace cravings with a feeling of ecstasy.

Keys to Success

Lesson thirteen: Give yourself a pat on the back.

Keys to Success

Lesson fourteen: Once you are comfortable with one Gum-day, try substituting two, and eventually three days out of the week.

CHAPTER SEVEN

Step Seven:
Increase Your
Drive

Now we must learn how to keep ourselves on those tiptoes.

Could you imagine working at a job in a world where managers didn't exist, with no one to watch over you and no one to keep you from becoming a lazy bag of-?

Even though it's humiliating to tell your friends and family that you are going to quit smoking for fear of backlash, just do it. Every Gum-day, tell one new person you've quit; let him or her be your watchdog. Go ahead and tell all your smoking partners not to offer you any more cigarettes unless you ask for one three times. I want you to beg and humiliate yourself; it's for your own good. If any of your smoking partners try to peer pressure you into smoking by offering you a cigarette, then practice saying no. If you can't say no when you quit for good then you are still not ready to quit.

For you to successfully quit, people need to know about it; you need to make yourself feel threatened and think "What if that person catches me? They will be so disappointed. I will just look like your typical powerless addict." It's true though; that is what they will think, and the more people who think this of you, the more your own "crying wolf" story will begin to haunt you. I always say the best way to learn a lesson is the hard, painful way because only then will you listen with both your heart and your mind. If you have not felt the strongest emotion of any kind when a lesson is to be taught, you will have nothing to remind you of what was just in front of you. The lack of an emotional reminder is part of why people continue to make mistakes in their everyday lives.

No one else can truly make you feel bad about smoking, but the thought of them being disappointed can assist you. This is your life; it's your habit, so it's up to you to kick those butts right out the door!

Keys to Success

    Lesson fifteen: Every Gum-day tell one new person you've quit.

Keys to Success
    Lesson sixteen: Have smoking partners only give you a smoke if you ask three times.

Keys to Success

Lesson seventeen: Practice saying no. It's up to you to kick those butts out the door.

CHAPTER EIGHT

Step Eight:
Jumping On and Off
the Bandwagon

EVENTUALLY YOU WILL COME TO find that you are like a lost lover with your cigarette, going back and forth like a break up-make up scene. Continue to quit completely on your Gum-day routines, only this time, do it without any nicotine suppressors. Go ahead and fail a time or two if you wish. Why? Because now I want you to enjoy each and every puff of every cigarette you inhale. Enjoy your cigarettes as if tomorrow never comes; as if this were your last cigarette.

The time has begun to start finding a hobby or lightly exercising for a replacement activity. You can take vitamins or eat vitamin rich foods for spiritual stabilization but I suggest you talk to your doctor before starting a vitamin program. Incorporate these changes while you're still a smoker; start working on any unhealthy eating habits too. When the time comes to quit cold turkey, you are going to have a lot of energy to burn as well as many other cravings you'll want to fill.

I mentioned this near the beginning of the book and it was taught to me by my brother who is a non-smoker. He said "I think in order for smokers to quit successfully, they need to replace their habit with something they enjoy equally as much." That to me, was a powerful statement and is the key that continues to resonate in my mind. It was also the motivation I personally needed to take that final step of never looking back.

If you are having difficulty replacing bad habits with good habits keep in mind that when you do something consistently for ten days, it will become a habit. Right now is the perfect time to start finding activities for any situation and turn it into a habit. Keep yourself busy at work or at home. Try to get in shape by learning to do simple things such as jumping rope, jumping jacks or jogging, which, like will power, are skills that can be acquired. Experiment with healthy snack foods like pita dipped in hummus, or various different kinds of fruits while drinking plenty of water each day. Straight tea of any kind is a great substitute that provides an herbal flavour of leaves, but more particularly green tea has a stronger body similar to the after taste of tobacco. Chamomile tea is another wonderful choice because it is a calming/relaxing tea to help un-wind wound up nerves. However, water is going to help you out the most! Water cleanses the body to help remove toxins caused by smoking, especially nicotine. When the day comes that you decide to kung fu your smoking addiction, water will reduce cravings and speed up your body's detoxifying process.

Earlier, I recommended vitamins because they increase the internal healing of your system while improving and stabilizing your mood. Vitamins that work in favour of the brain, such as Omega 3-6-9 or 5-htp, help to reduce mood swings for the first few days of cold turkey. The vitamins D and B are good for decreasing depression and stress which you may also experience the first few days. You can always visit your local health shop and speak to the clerk about which vitamin will suit your needs.

As I'm sure you're well aware eating habits and anxiety are the two most common concerns smokers have when looking to quit. If you do decide to use vitamins as an aid I suggest you start taking them 1-2 weeks before your set quit date.

You can conquer the final step without the use of vitamins, but if you are worried about physical or mental changes, these supplements can be used as a safe tool to help keep you balanced.

Keys to Success
    Lesson eighteen: Stop the use of suppressants on Monday's.

Keys to Success

Lesson nineteen: Enjoy every puff of every cigarette.

Keys to Success
    Lesson twenty: Search for new hobbies.

Keys to Success

Lesson twenty-one: Eat healthy, lightly exercise, and drink plenty of water.

CHAPTER NINE

Step Nine:
I Quit

FINALLY, AFTER MUCH HARD WORK and dedication, it arrives at your doorstep: will power. The days, weeks, months, and years spent training your brain to no longer need cigarettes and to say "no" have paid off; it is now time to pick your official quit date.

I would suggest quitting near the beginning or end of summer, mainly because you will be in much better spirits and also because you will have greater opportunities to burn that extra energy off. Let's not forget how much more challenging it will be to say "no" on a hot summer's day with a drink in hand. If you start off strong and tackle the most difficult trials first, the rest is downhill from there.

For this step you are no longer allowed to touch any nicotine of any kind; the gum you have? Throw it out! Write on your calendar what day you intend to quit; count down the days if you want to.

Most importantly, really enjoy your last pack of smokes. Talk to your cigarettes and tell them good-bye. Express all the fun times you've had and explain to them that it is now the end of their life to you instead of the end of your life because of them. On your last day of smoking, ration out your cigarettes; make sure all but two of them will be consumed by the end of the day. I left myself with two cigarettes inside their original package, and I placed them in the freezer (you can place them wherever you want as long as it's somewhere you will encounter them on a regular basis) just in case I wanted one, you know? Actually that's not the purpose; you will keep them there simply to reinforce the fact that it is all about will power. I did this literally to tempt me. I put them there so that every time I opened the freezer I could very well go back to smoking if I wanted to. I didn't though because it felt so much better to close the freezer door on what were once my two best friends. This helped to remind me of just how easy it is to say no and you really need to be reminded of that. It prepares you for everyday that you step outside of your home. In fact, both cigarettes are still sitting in my freezer!

Once you get through the first day, tell yourself "I survived day one; it's going to get easier from here." Pre-label your calendar for the month so that you can reward yourself with a big fat x for every day you succeed. After a few days you may not even care to give yourself an x anymore. You already know it's flat out over and done with.

For the first few weeks, chew an immense amount of long-lasting gum and buy yourself a litre of water every day to go nuts with. The other great benefit with water is that you can drink as much of it as you like and you will never have to feel guilty about it.

Naturally from time to time you may be tempted at the sight or smell of others smoking. When that happens, look up, down or all around. Find something else to focus your attention on until the craving subsides, or simply walk away.

These next tips are very important and should be followed for the first couple of days. Do not stand around having conversations with smokers on break. Only do this once you are confident that the smell of smoke and the association of socializing while smoking aren't going to affect you. Avoid in-depth conversations and long periods of standing with people for the first day or two. Interacting with people for extended periods may encourage eagerness, cravings, and a bitter, possibly offensive, attitude.

Every person is different, so time periods may vary. I had to avoid my dad who was my closest smoking buddy for a month. That was probably the most difficult challenge I encountered. Although, it wasn't terribly too bad as I got to reward myself with a little indulgence. I decided that for the first week only it is ok to binge, if you must, on sweet gummy bears, marshmallows, and cake with ice cream, but for one week only. After the first week, it is better to only reward your sweet tooth at the end of every successful week. Please make sure to enjoy and reward yourself every day of your first week. If you crave an expensive smoothie that is an hour's drive away, go get it! If you want to laugh hysterically for no reason and scream aloud, just do it; don't let anybody tell you otherwise. You've quit smoking, so go ahead and explore your new bouts of energy! Going for multiple walks and smelling the fresh air, either alone or with someone, is a great way to vent off steam and tire yourself out. I also recommend for your official quit date that you keep it a secret until you are certain that "this is it." I've found most people aren't very supportive. They usually mock you and say things like "yeah right I'll believe it when I see it" which may cause you to retaliate further.

Up until about day five, it is in your best interest to avoid hearing or saying the words "quit," "cigarette," "smoke," "nicotine"," or anything else related to smoking. Hearing those familiar terms may cause you to salivate slightly with a tempting desire. This will bring you un-necessary grief.

After your first month is done and over, remind yourself "I have accomplished this month without any form of nicotine; it's going to get easier from here." Keep your mind, body, and hands occupied at all times for the first little while; maybe carry a pen everywhere. If you are ever in doubt, never forget that all it takes for you to succeed is to quit cold turkey for three weeks. By then the nicotine will be completely out of your system and the rest from there is all about having the right frame of mind.

Keys to Success

Lesson twenty-two: Quit at the beginning or end of summer.

Keys to Success

Lesson twenty-three: Really enjoy your last pack of smokes. Talk to them.

Keys to Success

Lesson twenty-four: Set aside two cigarettes from your last pack and keep them somewhere you will encounter them on a regular basis.

Keys to Success
Lesson twenty-five: Keep your mind, body and hands occupied.

Keys to Success

Lesson twenty-six: Avoid socializing for the first few days.

Keys to Success

Lesson twenty-seven: Keep your quitting success a secret at first.

Keys to Success

Lesson twenty-eight: Chew lots of gum followed by plenty of water.

Keys to Success
    Lesson twenty-nine: Reward yourself daily by indulging in treats.

Keys to Success

Lesson thirty: You only have to be free of nicotine for three weeks.

CHAPTER TEN

Step Ten:

Good Luck

Congratulations! You have officially discovered the art to successfully quitting cold turkey. Although I cannot determine how successful your attempts will be, I will say good luck to a healthier future. If you are able to quit smoking cold turkey do something wonderful for yourself, save your pennies! All the money that you would have spent on a pack of smokes put it in a safe place and spend it once a week or once per month. After you are finished spoiling yourself save up for a nice trip. I rewarded my one year anniversary by hiking up a mountain with my new found energy and lung capacity.

If you find that you are still struggling after a few weeks but are able to be around people who smoke without feeling anxious, enjoy their second hand. It sounds gross but it is a guilt free way to eliminate minor cravings without giving up. Never forget that cigarettes are said to be just as difficult if not even more difficult than heroin to quit. If you can accomplish this I guarantee there will never be a challenge you can't overcome. That's a huge feat to conquer, a feat others will applaud. The choices you make affect the World. Your actions have the capability to influence others and reduce hazardous waste in the environment. Go on, be proud!

I have included a breakdown of all the key points at the end of this chapter for quick reference. There are also four pages of tips and tricks as well as two pages for notes where you can write any other information you've found to be helpful in this book. Never give up, prepare for the future and go at your own pace.

Remember, you could attempt to quit one million times but it only takes one of those tries to actually succeed. The main key is to never give up trying. Just because you failed today doesn't mean you can't try again tomorrow.

Keys to Success

Lesson thirty-one: Start saving your pennies.

Lessons at a glance

1. You must want to quit, discover the motivating factor and substitute it with something you enjoy equally as much.
2. You must earn willpower by taking thing's one day at a time. Start by telling every cigarette, one day you will quit.
3. Your cigarette does not own you; you own it.
4. You wear its effects clearly even when you try to hide it.
5. Start your day off without lighting up for one hour. Reduce how many cigarettes you smoke on break and or skip a smoke-break all together.
6. Don't smoke in the house or car.
7. Feel embarrassed and ashamed about smoking.
8. Wash the nicotine from your life.
9. Allow the guilt in and use it to build will power.
10. Substitute Monday's for Gum-day's.
11. Reward yourself with one smoke at the end of your Gum-day but only in the evening.
12. Replace cravings with a feeling of ecstasy.
13. Give yourself a pat on the back.

14. Once comfortable with one Gum-day try to substitute two days out of the week.
15. Every Gum-day tell one new person you've quit.
16. Have smoking partners only give you a smoke if you ask three times.
17. Practice saying no. It's up to you to kick those butts out the door.
18. Stop the use of suppressants on Monday's.
19. Enjoy every puff of every cigarette.
20. Search for new hobbies.
21. Eat healthy, lightly exercise, and drink plenty of water.
22. Quit at the beginning or end of summer.
23. Really enjoy your last pack of smokes, talk to them.
24. Set aside two cigarettes from your last pack and keep them somewhere you will encounter them on a regular basis.
25. Keep your mind, body and hands occupied.
26. Avoid socializing for the first few days.
27. Keep your quitting success a secret at first.
28. Chew lots of gum followed by plenty of water.

29. Reward yourself daily by indulging in treats.
30. You only have to be free of nicotine for three weeks.
31. Start saving your pennies.

Notes:

Notes:

10 Tricks to kill a craving

1. Chew gum.
2. Sing a song.
3. Eat chocolate, candy or fruit.
4. Drink tea, coffee or water.
5. Volunteer or enrol in an after work program.
6. Do a ten minute intense exercise.
7. Scream or laugh out loud.
8. Call a non-smoking friend or family member.
9. Draw, write or engage in crafts.
10. Keep yourself active and busy.

10 Easy ways to exercise

1. Skip rope or do 30 jumping jacks.
2. Run or jog.
3. Go for a walk.
4. Hit a speed bag or pillow.
5. Do some muscle stretching.
6. Ride a bicycle.
7. Play basketball, soccer or baseball.
8. Do breathing exercises.
9. Try Yoga, Pilates or Qigong.
10. Get a gym membership or buy equipment for your home.

10 Ways to reward yourself

1. Get an expensive breakfast, lunch or dinner.
2. Purchase a new cd or dvd.
3. Visit a spa.
4. Buy a new outfit.
5. Take a mini vacation.
6. Try something you weren't. able to do before because you smoked like hiking, sports etc.
7. Go out to a theatre and catch a new movie.
8. Look into the mirror and praise yourself.
9. Save up for something big like a new car, trip or any expensive item.
10. Indulge in whatever your new cravings tell you to.

Top 10 "What If's"

1. If a movie involves a lot of character's smoking watch half today and half tomorrow.
2. If you must stand with people who smoke bring a coffee, tea or water as your vice.
3. If your significant other smokes ask them politely not to do it around you.
4. If your parents smoke and it becomes tempting think about how much it hurts you to see them do this to themselves.
5. If you are studying and becoming frustrated take a break but try to stay in the 'study mood'.
6. If you get cravings while driving bring light snacks with you to munch on e.g. nuts, dried fruit, cold vegetables.
7. If you are having an argument with someone walk away until the feeling of wanting to smoke subsides.
8. If someone keeps trying to peer-pressure you think to yourself "maybe they are only doing this to ease their own conscious" and don't give in, some people will offer you a smoke just to see if you'll resist.

9. If you're visiting somewhere that allows smoking in public places, step outside and see how much you stink, also notice that all you can smell and taste is smoke. Give it an hour and you will find that water just doesn't quench the thirst of being dried up like a prune after the chemicals strip you down.

10. Lastly, if down the road you become tempted really think about all that you've accomplished, try to remember your life as a smoker and your life now. Think about how guilty you would feel if you were to forfeit this many years of success for what? Just one measly cigarette. Smoking is never worth risking your health or self-respect.

Epilogue

I HAD BEGUN SMOKING AT THE ripe age of eleven. Right around that age, a child's body is going through one of the biggest changes it may ever experience. When you start to pack it with 4000 chemicals per cigarette it's almost guaranteed there are going to be repercussions at some point. You are literally cutting off blood flow, depleting the brain of oxygen and impairing the growth of soft tissues. You're just creating damage before the body even has a chance to develop into being strong and healthy.

When I was 18 years old, the mucus production inside my lungs had increased to try and repair the damaged tissue; every day it felt like there was a risk of drowning at the mercy of my own body. By 20 years old, I was frequently ill with chest infections. I had sharp pains in my lower throat, followed by extremely painful and hoarse coughs that would sometime's last five terrifying months. I started to see that I wasn't going to be around much longer if I didn't address the situation. Every day, it felt like I had an inch worth of available lung left for oxygen. The rest felt like it was trapped in layer upon layer of tar.

By the time I reached 22 years of age, I became healthier, more active, and more motivated to give myself a life I had never dreamed of. I began working out by doing machine cardio exercise and weight training. A year later after my brother told me about that one golden rule of substitution I thought I could master something simple like skipping rope for ten minutes. I got two minutes into it and my lungs were on fire. A rash developed across my chest where my lungs lay, and I was hyperventilating like you wouldn't believe! That's when it hit me: I was about to turn 23 years old! We all like to make crude jokes and say we have the lungs of an 80–year-old, but in all honesty, what non-smoking 80-year-old will have lungs like mine? My guess is not many!

The point is, I realized the damage I had done and knew it was going to be now or never. After the first month of quitting, I decided to take an inhale of someone else's smoke. Once I had deeply inhaled and exhaled, I was certain that I could never touch another cigarette again; smoking is just something that is far too good to be true! The risk of getting hooked all over again is just too great and when you say goodbye, it has to be forever. Eventually at some point in your life when you are around smokers, even if it's outside the next day you will feel sick. I always dry up like a prune and wake up with sore throats. Plus, just as a reminder when I leave a party or something I'll sniff my hair or clothes, it smells utterly disgusting.

I hope my book was able to open your eyes and provide you with some useful tips. Keep an eye out for future books in the Quitting Cold series!

Appendix

Official Quitting Cold Site's
http://www.quittingcold.com
http://www.quittingcold.ca

Support Forum
http://www.whosready.com